RAILS THROUGH DIXIE

RAILS THROUGH DIXIE

JOHN KRAUSE
with H. REID

Golden West Books
San Marino, California

RAILS THROUGH DIXIE

THIS IS HOW IT HAPPENED

Almost every serious photographer will tell you that some day he plans to do a book. I have felt myself to be in this category for a long time and what is now presented herewith is the result of more than a score of years in which the railroad has been photographed from every angle — the main line, the logging railroad and the short line. Since my teens I have traveled the length and breadth of the United States in search of the steam locomotive and this, to me, has been a most rewarding hobby. Now that steam has vanished it occurred to me that my graphic chronicle could be shared with others, with a book as a vehicle. I have, through the years, seen railroad picture books come and go, a few to remain as classics. Even though the field may be saturated with coffee table books, furniture books and non-books, I hope that my offering may have something to give the reader delight and, perhaps, a memory and a railroad story picture. I readily admit that being a photographer does not always mean that one is a writer and author, and it is for this reason that I called in my good friends, H. Reid of Norfolk, Virginia, who collaborated in text and captions, and Donald Duke of San Marino, California, publisher of Golden West Books. I am deeply grateful to them. Their contribution helped to make *Rails Through Dixie* possible.

JOHN KRAUSE

THE END PAPERS

The scent of newly sawn logs hangs heavily in the moist air into which lavish amounts of coal smoke is added by Mower Lumber Company Shay No. 4 wending over winding rails above Cass, West Virginia. It was the make-do of equipment and the moil of men who didn't mind sweating in their workshirts that brought fortunes to unseen financiers in remote offices — and a living for the laborers in what the South looked upon as economy.

Golden West Books
P.O. Box 80250
San Marino, California • 91108-8250

Table of Contents

South of here Dixie begins — Reading No. 2100 on an Iron Horse Days special in 1964, heads for Washington, D.C. Baltimore & Ohio as well as Pennsylvania Railroad motive power units head out from the Capitol dome.

Preface

DIXIE BEGINS, certain geographers suggest, at round-house stall numbered one at Ivy City, Washington, District of Columbia.

Below this existed in steam railroad days a heartening camaraderie between passenger train crews and their patrons. In the backlands, where struggling, unheralded short lines clattered along on a languid schedule of freight service only, daily except Sunday, a close feeling of trainmen for cargo also manifested itself.

By the time their rattler pulled into the depot at the far end of the line, townsfolk hinted, the crew was on speaking terms with the l.c.l. chicks crated in the caboose.

Such informality and unhurried ways interested John Krause, Long Island electrical contractor. Time and time again, he had asked himself is it true what they say about Dixie?

In the late forties, Krause loaded holders for his Speed Graphic and headed south to find out. The knowing did not take long.

In 1949, Wadley, Georgia, was concerned about what could befall it such as holdover spies from World War II and also yankees.

At this time, Krause was young enough not to be able to afford a station wagon truck which he used to advantage on subsequent trips. At first, he traveled by train. He did the best he could in photographing the Sylvania Central, Wadley Southern and Louisville & Wadley by walking their tracks. One night at the depot, a representative of the law struck up a conversation. He wanted to know what the h - - - Krause was doing. A friend of the sheriff, attired in a blue suit with bright metallic buttons and a five starred ornament on the jacket, turned out to be an observant fellow. He confided he'd been tailing Krause all week.

"I've just been taking pictures of trains," said Krause, wondering if he should start whistling "Dixie."

"Your hobby?" said the sheriff.

"Yes, sir," said Krause. What else was there to say?

"That being the case," the man in blue said, "he'p yourself."

Which is what Krause did, only with the understanding that Wadley, Georgia, is always careful in case foreign agents might wish to harm its railroads.

In a few years, Krause had acquired the distinctive Dodge station wagon whose padlocks at side doors were as much standard equipment as some of the accessories—say, the tires, brakes and the like. He drove to Louisiana to photograph the Tremont & Gulf, where he found his up north ways a deterrent to picture permission.

"Why did you lock your car with padlocks?" the vice president and general manager asked. "Nobody hereabouts will bother anything."

Krause undid the locks, rolled down all of the windows and soon joined the honesty-conscious official who now felt a lot better about the whole thing. So did Krause.

All the while, he realized Southerners, initially aloof around strangers who might import alien gospel, are really a hospitable people. Railroaders, knowing all Krause wanted was to make pictures of their trains, obliged with smoke, the most, in instances, since the burning of Atlanta.

By now, he had assembled an extensive photographic coverage built solely on accuracy. His inviolate premise has always been to show trains in the area they serve. At first, his photography was for his own enjoyment, but when others became interested in his pictures, Krause insured there would be no distortion. If one is to introduce a train and its setting, one does not resort to falsifi-

cation such as the illusion of motion by means of intentional blurs or deploy a so-called candid feeling through calculated grain large as oats. Krause finds no fault with three-quarter frontal angles, although he experiments with others compatible with his original intent. There simply is no fraud in a Krause photograph.

Display of such quality work prior to this book, has been limited to contributions to magazines, calendars and others' hard covers.

Last year, Krause got together with Donald Duke of Golden West Books to initiate a layout for this volume, and high time somebody compiled a Krause anthology, I say. I also contend that the experienced Duke, a bit shrewd in beating other publishers to the draw, may have been surprised at Krause's attitude. The whole thing smacks of Krause's wanting to share his collection with collectors interested in sane photography. I know that he told Duke to use as many pictures as he could so folks would get their money's worth.

Krause's main worry was his relative anonymity.

"Nobody's ever heard of me," Krause said.

They will.

His pictures here will just about shriek John Krause.

The candid Krause was also upset about text.

"I guess I'm just a photographer," he told Duke.

Which is about where I came in.

Krause was beginning to send me letters about his regretting not having kept notes on his picture locations, of wishing he had traced Dixie engine biographies a little more closely and, finally, he out and out asked would I do the text for his picture book?

Duke flew in from the West Coast and Krause down from Long Island. We discussed the project, starting at a vintage Chesapeake Bay beach house built by a sea captain in 1907 of teak wood and tough as stone even today. In this atmospheric surrounding, I checked Krause's Dixie railroad material. I wanted to make certain it neither condemned nor flattered our land, but presented it as it was with perhaps a slice of whimsy which was, indeed, present. An examination of the pictures convinced me Krause had succeeded 100 per cent. Then came a series of cross country mail conferences, with postage fees running as much as five dollars a parcel—and there were several parcels.

Despite the distance handicap, communication was rapid and the work schedule relatively brief. As I had been to many of the places Krause photographed, research was that much ahead.

Those Southland locations Krause visited which you see here . . . Krause liked them and the South liked Krause.

H. Reid

Norfolk, Virginia
September 1965

7

1 - The Coast Lines

Rockton & Rion's No. 19, shorn of sentiment, was, like so many other Southland engines, a sound second-hand investment with which to move trains. There were some romanticists who opined the 2-8-2 also added perkiness to the South Carolina scene.

OVER THE salt-swathed crusts of the Atlantic Ocean sailed English adventurer Sir Walter Raleigh to colonize in 1585 the new land on the bleached sands of the Outer Banks that has become North Carolina. The settlers, after Raleigh's return to the mother country, disappeared. They left no positive trace, although beachcombers hundreds of years later, stirred up guesses with the finding of bits of jagged earthenware and rust-crusted slivers of hammered metal. What became of the band may never be solved. It is one of history's greatest enigmas. Other homesteaders braved the wild seas and uncertainties of the uncharted New World in the 1650's. Their land, rising from the pinetopped east, to the red clay of the Piedmont and the stony steeps of the West, developed into a British invasion point during the Revolution.

Later, it became one of the original 13 states and subsequently a member of the Confederacy, whose demise doomed the ruling plantation system.

Needing a device to support the evolution of farm tenancy, the historically wealthy Tar Heel State looked to its burgeoning railroads, some of which were small indeed, but nearly a century later, as steam power wafted from the old South, the little lines measured, in a way, equally as large as the Class I's.

Among the regional routes whose pictures appear herein are the Cone Mills' towel road, the Cliffside daubed in a cleansing charm all its own; the Rockingham in the area of sand and hillock; the Winston-Salem Southbound, going pell mell through the Piedmont; the Durham & Southern, another racer in the midlands, and the Virginia & Carolina Southern, an Atlantic Coast Line cousin just above the border of South Carolina, another of the original 13 states dating back to the 16th Century exploration.

The Palmetto State was visited by Spaniards in 1526, while the English founded Charleston in 1680. Cotton and tobacco crops flourished until the Civil War — South Carolina was the first to secede from the Union (December 20, 1860). Like the Carolina above it, South Carolina needed postbellum railroading to support its economy and crop diversification. By World War I, a successful transition was reached with the local lines, again serving suitably.

Among those featured here working steam into a later era: the Bennettsville & Cheraw in textile and farm country; the quarry road of Rockton & Rion, and the lumber-associated Hampton & Branchville.

Even more Souther'd in traditional Dixie were the Georgia lines, the Sylvania Central of which there shall never be a sequel; the Louisville & Wadley and companion Wadley Southern; Wrightsville and Tennille and Live Oak, Perry & Gulf, more often shown in Florida locations. All of these were the Georgia lines wending virtually unnoticed through the pines in the largest state east of the Mississipi, one that produces from those trees half of the world's naval stores. These railroads were the struggling corporations in the post-Sherman era that hauled the product processed in the cotton engine (i.e., cotton gin). Those earthy corporations, rising from the boggy, woody Atlantic coastal plains to the broad midsection to the northeast mountains, cast their begrimed lot in the wake of explorer De Soto, there in 1540, and James Oglethorpe who founded Savannah in 1733. Still, the Georgia roads, along with so many of the South's others, gained recognition only at the next station down the weedy tracks, rather than on a national scope.

Running in such storied land, they toiled nigh nameless in Dixieland save for a line or so of type in the Official Guide of Railways.

VIRGINIA BLUE RIDGE

In Thomas Jefferson country, the Virginia Blue Ridge Railway outlasted a malady decimating its principal commodity — timber — and displayed more courage of sorts by retaining steam power far longer than most. In the view above, No. 6, a former Southern Railway freight mover at Union, South Carolina, and on Virginia's Keysville Branch, takes cars from the American Cyanamid plant at Piney River. Of a design gaining popularity during World War II, six-wheel switcher No. 9, at the left, leaves the Tye River wye, fastens to its train, then returns to home quarters at Piney River. (LOWER LEFT) The No. 9 is coupled to a wagon top box car showing effects of having come from VBR's best customer which trades in titanium, the ingredient that makes white paint white.

The 0-6-0, having gone under Highway 29, now bites into an upgrade en route to a Tye River meeting with the Southern Railway. (BELOW) The No. 6 after its Virginia Blue Ridge days, made a strong comeback in New Jersey with excursion-minded Morris County Central.

E. J. LAVINO

In livery of royal blue with yellow trim, E. J. Lavino's tank switcher escorts a hot car to the slag dump at Reusens, Virginia, just outside of Lynchburg, near the Chesapeake & Ohio's James River line. The 0-6-0, built to World War II Transportation Corps lines, is equipped with built-up auxiliary headlight to reach above the molten waste car whose contents, when tilted out, resemble a phosphorescent tomato soup, only much, much hotter. Shipping firm Lavino operates hard metal plants at Reusens and Sheridan, Pennsylvania. Each plant ran steam switchers.

CAROLINA SOUTHERN

Carolina Southern 2-6-0 No. 100, with push pole prominent on pilot deck, wibbles and wobbles from Ahoskie to Windsor, North Carolina. Interchange was with the Atlantic Coast Line at Ahoskie. C. S. — the Siesta, as it was sometimes called — was an outgrowth of a line that, curiously enough, owned a narrow gauge Atlantic type.

ROCKINGHAM

Plumb at the bottom of North Carolina is Rockingham, whose Atlantic Coast Line relationship is more than implied. No. 935, in the view above, is unmistakably an inheritance from ACL, while the Gibson, North Carolina, depot bears the purple color scheme in past favor by the larger concern. The wooden caboose, metal awnings capping its windows, was previously Coast Line-owned. At the right, the 10-wheeler whizzes along on firm roadbed of the 20-mile route between Rockingham and Cheraw, South Carolina. Lumber products, contributing largely to Rockingham's income, do not reflect in the day's consist. The locomotive will be coaled from a hillside ramp in a deep cut tucked away in downtown Rockingham, a grouping of 4,000 denizens who have in their midst an inn hosted by Gil Coan, in his day a stellar outfield operative for the old Washington baseball Senators.

WINSTON-SALEM SOUTHBOUND

The question most posed to railroaders on the Winston-Salem Southbound was what happened to all the steam trains once they went South? They did return the 90 miles from Wadesboro to Winston-Salem, North Carolina, but the southlanders weren't a-talking about it in the corporate title. The Southbound No. 300, a 1925 Baldwin shown above, takes coal at the High Rock connection with High Point, Thomasville & Denton. The No. 301, at the right, steals through an uncommon rockbound path of the Carolina Piedmont flatlands.

At the left, Winston-Salem Southbound No. 400, once Norfolk & Western chattel, emits exhaust snappily in a romp through Piedmont, North Carolina. The N&W sold the Winston-Salem line its No. 1393 Mallet on June 14, 1941. (ABOVE) Southmont is 31.9 miles from the tobacco sales center of Winston-Salem line. It is also the site of a blind grade crossing, a holdover from the horse and buggy days when denizens leisurely went to Southmont depot to see the Southbound's trains steaming north. (RIGHT) In latter steam days, the Winston-Salem Southbound 2-8-2's were preferred for the faster run across High Rock Lake and through Cotton Grove, Lexington and the hospitable hamlet with name to match — Welcome, North Carolina.

DURHAM & SOUTHERN

One of the goingest freight lines in the Tar Heel state, Durham & Southern, exhibited decided preference for Decapods for its 56.8 miles between Durham and Dunn extremities. The No. 403, a 1929 Baldwin procured from the Alabama, Tennessee & Northern, shown in the upper left, flies the white flags of an unscheduled move in May 1950 at Dunn, and is a well groomed Durham & Southern example. (ABOVE) The 1933 Baldwin-built No. 202 was fleet indeed, and made a mile-a-minute with far more tonnage than this 1952 consist at Dunn. On the left, No. 403, handled by a pleasant chap waving the time of day, makes for Durham & Southern outposts at Few, Carpenter, Upchurch, Apex and Coats. (BELOW) Praise be, a young gentleman at Dunn pedals his wheel closer to the No. 202 in perpetuating a custom of his elders: watching the trains come in.

ATLANTIC & WESTERN

To get anywhere, one needs connections. The Atlantic & Western went 24 miles from Sanford to Lillington via Jonesboro, North Carolina, in order to make connections with the right people: Seaboard, Atlantic Coast Line, Norfolk Southern and just plain Southern, yet the A&W missed the privilege status. (UPPER LEFT) The day No. 9 ran this train was the norm Atlantic & Western would have liked. (ABOVE) The heat of the day is upon the No. 9, as rails creak out complaints. (LOWER LEFT) The push-pull turntable and the corrugated shed eaten orange from aggravating rust are hidden in the business section of Sanford. The No. 12, a 1911 Baldwin, came to the A&W from Norfolk Southern where it had been the No. 203, and from Raleigh & Southport which had numbered it as No. 10. The old Atlantic & Western motor car is a decaying reminder of busier commerce.

HIGH POINT, RANDLEMAN, ASHEBORO & SOUTHERN

While the heads of milk weeds nod in the trace of a breeze, the No. 516 of the High Point, Randleman, Asheboro & Southern churns up a minor hurricane from its stack in departing High Point, North Carolina, America's furniture capital. The 2-8-0 is a Southern heritage. The HPRA&S was incorporated in 1883, but it wasn't until 1887 anyone did anything about it.

BUFFALO & UNION-CAROLINA

Buffalo & Union-Carolina 10-wheeler No. 3, its boiler jacket fading from its once dazzling green paint, passes an observant weed-chopping crew and a sturdy pig sty off to the other side. The South Carolina road shuttled a single bob-tailed tender between its pair of locomotives.

CLIFFSIDE RAILROAD

Textile wares at Cliffside, North Carolina, were dispatched to the Seaboard at Cliffside Junction, calculated three miles distant, in the tow of green and orange-yeller No. 110, a smart looking Prairie type. Not far down the road is Forest City, home of veteran major league baseball player Forrest Burgess, who, like the No. 110, was called Smoky. (LEFT CENTER) Engineer Odell Biggerstaff believed in protocol. "I just work here," he would allow, between drags on a high-tone cigar. "Now, I don't really have authority to pose the engine here and there, but if you've come such a far way, I'll slow 'er down for you." When the pace got to be zero miles an hour, everybody was happy. (ABOVE) The No. 110's tender was once home for a brood of chicks, each named for an official of Cone Mills, whose towel products could be purchased in town by the pound rather than piecemeal. (LEFT) Biggerstaff, of a morning, would place the engine near the town well, the water in which was as clear as a gambler's mind and twice as cool. Along about one in the afternoon, the goodly fellow would point toward Cliffside Junction in the attractive Vulcan that later was given a false stack but a new job — hauling tourists on the Swamp Rabbit Railroad at Cleveland, South Carolina.

VIRGINIA & CAROLINA SOUTHERN

In the sandlands of North Carolina, the Virginia & Carolina Southern never got to Virginia and went only 27 miles south, but the name sounded good anyway. (LEFT) Running on the main line at Hope Mills and bound for Lumberton is the Very Careful & Slow's No. 35, a 10-wheeler inherited from the Atlantic Coast Line. (ABOVE) Hunters and train crew discuss the day's quarry while the iron steed and dogs mark time. (LOWER LEFT) The Virginia & Carolina Southern assemblage of problems excluded those of fuel machine failures. Water and coal loaded at St. Paul went in by foolproof gravity. The riddle of the No. 33 is revealed: yes, it is on the track and, no, it is not moving more than 10 miles an hour.

BENNETTSVILLE & CHERAW

South Carolina's Bennettsville & Cheraw once ran three daily trains between Kollock and Sellers. Service was greatly curtailed by the 1950's when B&C 10-wheeler No. 31, shown below, waged a losing battle against obsolescence. Though the tumbledown shed purports little to outsiders, it was once a source of wonderment to the young of Bennettsville, for it was here that the B&C brought in the secrets from the far off places they heard their elders talk about in the parlor of the white-columned hotel in front of which were stately magnolias. Inside the hostelry lingered heartening accounts of bravery of the boys in gray billeted there in years past. The Bennettsville & Cheraw, long refusing to be ousted from the new South, gracefully vanished, but the memory of the No. 31 bringing in things from the stores up north is as indelible to some in Bennettsville as the musty old inn, the courthouse and the white church on the corner.

ROCKTON & RION

In this humble farmland, Southland's respected Furman University began. It is now removed to a point outside of Greenville, South Carolina, far from the putterings of Rockton & Rion's No. 19, a judicious purchase from a Birmingham iron firm. In the scene below, with extra provisions aboard the tender, the 2-8-2 switches just across the road from a remaining educational facility, Greenbrier High School. (RIGHT) At Anderson Quarry, alternate engine No. 712, once a dandy on the Atlantic Coast Line, is stored while No. 19 lights out for the morning granite train. Beyond Rion crush quarry, the No. 19, at the far right, takes the first installment of its load uphill to eventual transfer to the Southern Railway. The cast of a shortline was molded by those in the community. While the No. 19's master of the moment (LOWER RIGHT) hardly outdoes the Century's Bob Butterfield, he means infinitely more to the Rockton-Rion. Besides, the railroad wasn't the sort of line on which brightly illuminated Pullmans raced the clock, rather were paced wisely to allow a nap at noontime lunch hour.

About mid-point on the 12-mile Rockton & Rion, No. 19 pushes a gondola into place for a load of world-famous Winnsboro blue granite. Another buy from Woodward Iron in Alabama, the No. 31, shown below, bounds into the intermediate quarry yards in one of the all-too-few steam shows carrying into the mid-sixties.

A Rockton & Rion switcher backs up to a deep excavation for another exportation of the granite advertised as "The Silk of the Trade" and in demand as memorial markers. Though the 0-4-0 in the view above may not look like it, the tanker is, after a fashion, in Tombstone Territory. (RIGHT) Laborers in the metal trough whisk up from tending the scrap dump switcher to the steam crane on what unquestionably is one of the heaviest ballasted tracks in the entire world. When the discard blocks drop into place at the end of the line, the earth quivers, and trees, should they be in the way, splinter to smithereens.

GEORGIA & FLORIDA

In the pines, in the pines, where the sun seldom shines, is where Georgia & Florida's mixed hides and winds. Passengers in the rear car, divided because of the central baggage compartment, could pass the time of day with some degree of convenience while the Baldwin 10-wheeler uncoupled to switch freight cars, but then, Southerners knew how to go easy. Rushing about, do you think this 1910 vintage engine would have lasted so long? People are endangered of running out of steam, too, they know.

HAMPTON & BRANCHVILLE

Making way for a most worthy locomotive, Hampton & Branchville Nos. 32 and 44 take siding near the Lightsey lumber mill at Miley, South Carolina, in May 1950. For uncommon content, this might be considered as one of the outstanding photographs of the time, especially in view of hospitality never quite measuring to full amount amongst some echelons of Hampton & Branchville management. Disciples of olden steaming things maintained an aloofness from space explorations. (UPPER RIGHT) If Hampton & Branchville's bulbous chimnied No. 105 switched logs for the man in the moon, there might have been ardent lunar exploration converts. (OPPOSITE) Steam operations on the Hampton & Branchville, a lumber stretch of 14 miles built in 1890 and made a common carrier in September 1892, ended with the No. 44, a natty 4-6-0.

SYLVANIA CENTRAL

In the slight slopes of Georgia, the Sylvania Central once scurried. (BELOW) Its tried and true Baldwin 10-wheeler, built March 1905, contrasted with the new fangled contrivances it met at the Central of Georgia interchange. (RIGHT) The No. 103's 56-inch drivers flirt with irksome flora in winging along to Sylvania from Rocky Ford. The Sylvania Central "Flyer" was constructed originally for the Stillmore Air Line. Of the Central, photographer Krause casually remarked: "There is nothing left like the Sylvania Central." Enlarging on that, one might brashly conclude there never was anything like the Central before, either.

LOUISVILLE & WADLEY
WADLEY SOUTHERN

The good Lord looked down upon the red clay of Georgia and envisioned it as an edifying place to let things grow — tobacco, cotton, corn and tanglesome ninnie-weeds that clung to the rails of the 10-mile railroad, the Louisville & Wadley and neighboring Wadley Southern, strung out to facilitate hauling the money-making crops to market. For those persons who wished to take advantage of an Old South means of transit, the mixed train, they had but to repose in the car at the end, devoid of air conditioning which would have spoiled the savor of the 10-wheeler No. 41's coal smoke, journal oil and the sounds of birds on the wing. Helping guide the L&W's modest destinies were the Central of Georgia and the Louisville Fertilizer & Gin Co. — and the companion railroad, Wadley Southern, whose equipment was regularly borrowed. The Wadley Southern claimed revenue on the 19.8 miles from Wadley to Swainsboro.

On this misty day of 1956, with the Wadley Southern's steam activities already lapsing into the haze of time, the on-loan No. 41 leads a mixed over the literal undulations of the countryside unblemished with cuts and fills. While the track may have been less than perfect, then so, too, was the roadway at the right. Here was a pioneer life on the wane, a way oft ridiculed by unthinking and unknowing editors schooled in the ways of mass transportation. What they overlooked was the Georgians getting the most of their investments with far, far less capital to draw upon than available Class I railroads.

Dual duty No. 41, shown above, is fixing to be turned on the table smack in the middle of Swainsboro, Georgia, sidetrack. (RIGHT) On the Wadley Southern, the No. 41 crests a sandy mound by the depot. (LOWER RIGHT) The Wadley Southern's mixed, this time on Wadley Southern trackage using the Louisville & Wadley's No. 41 engine, goes on, on, on away from here. While there are yellowed albumen prints stowed among hand-stitched quilts in attic trunks, or as long as the aging summon whimsy from their broad memory — and as happenstance would have a stranger with a Speed Graphic in the midst, the classic Georgia convenience may not have, after all, steamed completely out of the Dixie picture.

And on the seventh day, the Louisville & Wadley and Wadley Southern, having Christian influences, rested at the Wadley, Georgia, shops, suffering the erosion of many seasons.

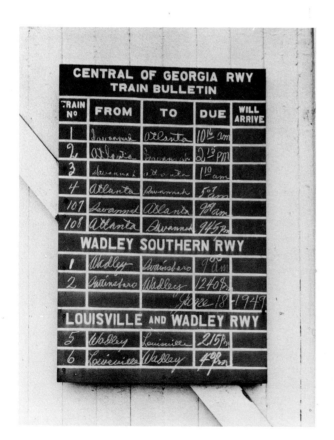

Wadley Southern No. 53 pulls up to the water plug for a long drink of water following a short soda pop stop by members of the crew.

Here's what enlivened a town such as Wadley . . . the 1904 Baldwin No. 53 of the Wadley Southern shown at the left, whose crew leans against the baggage cart being filled with store bought chicks, some Mason jars for the store and a tricycle for the little redheaded boy who lives behind the corn patch at the left of the locomotive. Already, news of this important event is being relayed by his older brother who pumps his two-wheeler past a parked blue '37 Ford upon whose fenders globs of orange mud are caked from yesterday's squall. Like the rural weekly newspaper, the train bulletin at the far left may not always have been devoted to punctuality.

WRIGHTSVILLE & TENNILLE

Wrightsville & Tennille's No. 213 smokes up Tennille, Georgia, in June 1949 while at the tank crusted with scum and algae of leaking water. The No. 213 and its rattler are a remnant of a more ambitious schedule of the Wrightsville & Tennille (those in the shire pronounced the second name to rhyme with kennel). Once, there was the 71.1-mile, two trains daily Tennille District to Hawkinsville with the high flown towns of Peacocks and Condor on the way. The 30.7-mile Eastman District, branching out from Dublin, 36.3 miles from Tennille, counted No.'s 5 and 6 each day.

LIVE OAK, PERRY & GULF

Live Oak, Perry & Gulf — famed for its cabbage stacked dar-
lings dieting on turpentine knots — ran a coal-fired 10-wheeler
quite similar to South Georgia's own. LOP&G No. 102 stands
by on the South Georgia at Adel, Georgia.

2 - Appalachia

In mountainous setting big as all outdoors — maybe larger — Mower Lumber Company Shay No. 4 comes out of the second switchback on Cheat Mountain in West Virginia, the land just beyond Dixie.

WEST VIRGINIA is a hilly state in the Allegheny Plateau, full of narrow valleys, gorges, wind gaps, waterfalls, logged-over mountains and dark-as-dungeon coal mines — and an array of modest railroads gamely retaining steam locomotives, ofttimes because none others could be paid for. The province was explored by 18th Century fur trappers and settled by Virginians who made it a part of the Old Dominion until the 1859 John Brown Raid changed all that. West Virginia was divided in loyalty during the internal conflict of the 1860's, emerging as a state separate from Virginia in 1863.

West Virginia relied heavily on timber and mineral commerce, moved eventually by companies depicted in this volume: Middle Fork, Cherry River Boom & Lumber Company, Buffalo Creek & Gauley, Meadow River Lumber Company, Mower Lumber Company, and a strange outgrowth of this defunct firm, the Cass Scenic Railway which borrows the old right-of-way in waiting upon tourists dwelling on the past.

Also in the pseudo-Dixie is Maryland, where Messrs. Dixon and Mason drew in the 1760's a line regarded as definitive separation of South from North. Running in the West Virginia side of Maryland, a state of 1632 origins at the behest of Lord Calvert, was the Preston, a coal railroad whose informalities doubled for deeper Southland's.

Also in mountainous terrain were the Morehead & North Fork and the Kentucky & Tennessee, servile to mined products of Kentucky, the state admitted to the Union in 1792 and whose obligations were split during the Civil War. Kentucky experienced dissonance in trade union sentiment in the 1930's, particularly in Harlan County, but found harmony in the generation of a folk music bearing the nickname of the state — Bluegrass.

In Tennessee, an area inspected by De Soto in 1540, claimed by Indians until the 1700's, and by individualists after the Revolution who for a time named the state Franklin, ran the legendary East Tennessee & Western North Carolina narrow as well as standard gauges, the waif Smoky Mountain, and the coal and forest-oriented Brimstone. These roads steamed in territory where, second only to Virginia, the bloodiest Civil War engagements were fought.

In the ridges of North Carolina, dealt with in detail in these pages, are the wee Black Mountain line and the lumber-totin' Graham County whose saga ranks among the all-time galluptious.

PRESTON RAILROAD

Preston Railroad's No. 18, shown at the upper right, accelerates with Baltimore & Ohio hoppers out of Crellin, Maryland, where Lord Baltimore's bailiwick and West Virginia boundaries play footsie. The road's No. 19, in the view above, a cap-stacked 2-8-0, moves toward a B&O transfer at the state line. The PRR emblazoned in the Crellin shop window shown above denotes Preston Railroad, the standard railroad of this coal area that in more lucrative times extended from Crellin to Hutton, Maryland, to Schaffer, West Virginia, a distance of 24 miles. (OPPOSITE) By the time No. 19 headed toward the B&O, total mileage was considerably reduced on the railroad whose destinies had been carefully woven by a closely knit group: S. A. Kendall, president; J. L. Kendall, vice-president; S. A. Kendall Jr., vice president, and J. W. Kendall, general manager. There was another ranking officer, the superintendent, a gentleman by the name of Kendall — J. L. Jr.

MIDDLE FORK RAILROAD

Ostensibly, a Middle Fork Heisler shown above, in remote Ellamore, West Virginia, near decaying trees and a withering economy, should be smoking bravely into obscurity. Strangely, the tide and corporate taxes were more predictable. The engine, whose owner was favorably disposed to antiques, cheated the scrapper's torch. The Heisler was dispatched to an unlikely point of exhibition, Little Washington, North Carolina. Its passage there was turbulent. The engine broke a drawhead in tow on the Chesapeake & Ohio. A hurricane accompanied its barged passage across Hampton Roads en route to a rail connection south.

In a land unspoiled by neon, billboards and parking meters, the Middle Fork Heisler, the last constructed, moves into position to transport four loaded hoppers. (UPPER RIGHT) With a furious roar, the No. 7 makes off with the late afternoon local wonder. (OPPOSITE) The No. 7 brings moderate business to the Baltimore & Ohio as the agent, about to check car numbers, leaves the comfort of a station whose mien is nigh on to unbelievable. (LOWER RIGHT) With a stranger in the midst, the wooden box car amongst the coal cars lends an even more fairy tale bearing to the whole of the Middle Fork.

Laced with snow, Ellamore, West Virginia, was home station for Moore Keppel
& Company's No. 6 shown at left. The Climax upon occasion was deputized for
the Middle Fork Heisler. Firebox cold, worn out Climax No. 3 stands useless in
the weeds on the ridge track. A prerequisite for activating any geared engine in
West Virginia was the placement of a bucket of lubricant on the pilot beam, and
though the Moore Keppel is putting on quite a show, there is a gaudy scene
stealer billed as Esso upstaging all else.

Looking back on it all, there is a Middle Fork trainman who knows his
engine is running on borrowed time, but it was certainly a long-term loan.

CHERRY RIVER BOOM & LUMBER

In an alpine clime where the humdrum got to be dang near fabled in editor Jim Comstock's weekly newspaper, Cherry River Boom & Lumber Co.'s Shay No. 7, just out of Richwood, West Virginia, festoons the skies with a blackened garland. A workaday quest for lumber on a system once knowing the bustle of 16 engines over 75 miles of track would always rate something special in The Hillbilly, the journal of genial Jim, a sort of headland Bret Harte. Writing with wit as dry and brittle as the soda crackers in red and white waxed wraps at general stores to which he gravitated in penning his Comstock's Lode column, the lank scrivener enjoyed chronicling trains of the land he fancied. Somewhere, sometime amongst the back issues — an index would spoil the adventure of it — one could read about Cherry River Boom & Lumber's prime era of steaming into 200,000 acres of virgin woodland in the counties of Nicholas, Greenbrier, Webster and Pocahontas. The trains began running regularly in July of 1901. Richwood was incorporated later — in November. With the railroad aiding immeasurably, the forestry-centered town was on its way to an annual output of nearly 6,000 cars of spruce and hemlock, paper, broom handles, chair rounds and wooden dishes. If one looked long enough through The Hillbilly, the detailed history of Richwood would be there in snappy prose (one of the largest industries was a clothespin factory). Comstock's homey paper followed a maxim identical to that of a rather well known metropolitan daily to the north: "All the news that's fittin' to print."

On the left, Cherry River Boom & Lumber Shay No. 7 lugs empties through thickets primeval. The work train in the center view follows a rail bus up branch to the August 1956 operations.

Two hay burners and a coal burner at the lower left remove hardwoods in the last CRB&L steam operations in the boondocks. (BELOW) Rod engine No. 15 heads up Cherry River for morning chores. Rails aboard flat cars are for the loader and tend to be less than perfect gauge.

In 1952, the No. 7 headed a woods train. The town of Richwood in the view below fell prey to the Depression, but the lumber company kept at it, providing continued solvency for a great many.

MOWER LUMBER COMPANY

In more volatile times at the logging town of Cass, West Virginia, life was band saw, bean tins and bedding down, preferably with the belle who knew best how to cope with a cosmic urge. By the time the Mower Lumber Co. Shay, on the left, helped close out woodcutting in 1960, the demeanor of the community lapsed into a tired tranquility. With the main saw mill shut down, Cass' population dwindled from the lusty 2,000 of a half a century before to a discouraged 300. Cass, the grouping of three log houses and 173,000 acres of red spruce, yellow birch and hard maples, had experienced phenomenal growth to include within its boundaries a supply store counting a million dollars in receipts yearly, several restaurants, a hotel caring for 75 guests, three churches, an unrecorded number of saloons, two schools and numerous residences as well as an output of 35 million board feet of wood plus pulp. Then, the boom town boomeranged. Lumber played out. The dozen logging Shays (including a 150-tonner, the heaviest ever built) were about all gone, steel was ripped out of the seven-mile Cheat Mountain Line. So steep had it been — four and five percent with some rises measured at 11 percent — that two switchbacks had been necessary. Now, all this was outmoded, even if the timber supply had held. Already, Spruce, a neighboring community 3,853 feet up and most accessible by rail, had shuttered its hotel and store, and sealed its post office permanently. Terminated, too, were five coal mines up there, but, then, some people, in considering the worth of the product, thought maybe this was just as well. Cass, itself, faced an exodus clop-clopping down its plank sideways until, strangely, the very obsolescence of the logging railroad checked it. Why not, the legislature proposed, capitalize on the old timey locomotives and rebuild them and the tracks as a tourist attraction? The minority of reluctant solons, viewing returns on the re-created Cass Scenic Railroad in the first season of 1962, rued delay in support. The old Shays nobody wanted at the town most everybody forgot brought in 23,000 persons during the opening 73 days.

55

Mower Lumber No. 4 takes water just beyond the mill.

Grammarians may frown on the spelli
above, but the message got across to the

Primitive equipment? Conceded it won none of Mister Pulitzer's prizes, although
much of Mower's logging apparatus remained functional for over a half-century.

No. 4 precedes its load on a
zagging track arrangement

e last word on the sign shown Mower No. 1.

Up from Harry Gum's farm, it was picturesque though a stiff workout for the Shay.

ain near one of the switchbacks, a zig- the absolute grade for the engine.

After a day in the woods, No. 4's train crew did justice to the elaborate dinners at Mrs. Ollie Erwin's boarding house at Cass.

No. 1, once painted Chinese red in the logging era, plugs along on the line that, even on the descent, seemed as though it were up all the time. (BELOW) The company truck is turned on a simple yet effective table.

CASS SCENIC RAILROAD

Shays Nos. 7 and 4, shown above, race a fuming thunderhead back to Cass where those in business related to tourism could see only brightness. Another excursion, on the left, shows Shays Nos. 7 and 5 in uncommon position. Normally, they pushed open-air cars. The average vacationer was less likely to be bothered with live cinders that way. For engineer Clyde Galford, a Shay man all his life, the new tourist trains differed from his free-wheeling past, but, by Ned, it was sporting to hear those gears whiz around again.

ELY-THOMAS LUMBER

Ely-Thomas Lumber Co. Shay No. 2 moves a load of dressed lumber at Fenwick, West Virginia, in 1963. The engine exhausted by way of a rather stout egress in the scene above. One of the E-T narrow gauge Shays, the No. 6, was thoughtfully preserved for tourist service at Allaire State Park near the New Jersey town owning up to the quaint name of Squankum. One of the new masters of the three-footer is a newspaperman turned engineer, Steve Ward, born well after most lumber companies abandoned rail methods. Yet, anachronistic Ward's touch on the throttle is as firm and sure as old Leon Davis, back when the dean of E-T engineers rolled logs out of a camp claiming an odd name, too: Jetsville.

Between moves, holdovers from the narrow gauge days swap recollections while aboard standard gauge Shay No. 2, a remnant itself from the old empire of Ralph Ely and Wellington Thomas, respected lumbermen whose campus at Werth, West Virginia, has won neatness awards. Werth was a coined word. It borrowed portions of the names of the two men.

It's rainin', rainin' here this morning, and No. 2 backs past a frame building showing festive yellow through the gloom at Fenwick in 1958 before alterations to the tender and number plate.

On a faired off 1958 day, Shay No. 2 passes a red on-line box car. (RIGHT) Ely-Thomas No. 2 in August 1956 works under a co-operative arrangement with the Baltimore & Ohio and Cherry River Boom & Lumber Company upon whose line the loader and train are halted.

ELK RIVER COAL & LUMBER

Elk River Coal & Lumber Co., in Clay County of West Virginia, long ago felled a poplar 88 feet to the first limb at Buffalo Fork. In tapping the once bountiful natural resources, the Elk River tracks pierced an expanse so wild, claimed idle guests on wintry nights at the matchless hostelry called Henry Clay at Clay, West Virginia, that the good Lord Himself might get lost at Buffalo Fork unless He consulted a map — if, perchance, He were lucky enough to find a chart with Clay County printed on it. The Elk River railroad's tracks lay submerged under mountain streams, hacked clear by axe in icy months. In blossom time, wild boar roamed at will, challenging anon the Elk River pufferbellies.

Elk River's Climax No. 3, shown above, last to log in the United States, and Shay No. 19, later to bear Georgia-Pacific heraldry, steam through The Big Woods. The No. 3 was purchased by a vacationer enterprise, the Carroll Park & Western near Bloomsburg, Pennsylvania, and converted to different gauge. Thus, the No. 3 enjoys the distinction of sole rank in functional four-foot passenger hauling Climaxes in this and any other country. (RIGHT) Waiting for clearance at a juncture with the Buffalo Creek & Gauley, a crewman utilizes Prince Albert's aromatic leaf in rolling his own. (LOWER RIGHT) Shay No. 19, bedecked with white extra flags on the BC&G main, makes its first trip into the woods. On the previous day, Shay No. 12 ran its last. While both engines were under steam at the Swandale mill, whistle farewells were sounded. The tones, it is hinted, were sadder than usual, but the lumbermen's emotions may have sounded the colossal note on that occasion.

Elk River Shay No. 12, an erstwhile Coal & Coke Railroad four-wheel bobber mixed in with log cars, backs into the Swandale mill in 1957. Immediately above, the Swandale mill pond and No. 12 with precious few more miles to go.

The handsome portrait shown below is the essence of Elk River's railroading: Shay No. 12 paused on a ford for water, trees, more trees, and the friend to all, Brooks Litton seated upon the tender. It was a fateful Thursday in May 1958, for the next day Shay No. 19 took over until the line itself was withdrawn. An English artist based this very photograph for an oil gaining much favor amongst rail buffs. (LEFT) Woods conductor Brooks Litton, at the left, checks loading arc of former steam apparatus changed over to motor power. The amiable young man, earnest about his work and yet possessed with a puckish sense of humor, once divulged that one of the main things he hoped God would do for him was to fix it so he would be able to work around log trains until he died. A week later, runaway logs crushed the likeable Litton. He had lived a short but full and happy life. (FAR LEFT) Sunshine slants through coal smoke hanging heavily in the forest.

Raymond Davies heard a noise that should not have been — ash pan was falling off. The matter was corrected after short delay. (RIGHT) In an episode so alien to dreadfully efficient Class I speed runs, Elk River Climax No. 3 breasts a torrent while a nonchalant group finds nothing out of ordinary. They'd been here before and, besides, tomorrow might be worse.

Track workers create a new avenue for timber trains with artist Phil Ronfor observing intently from a flat car. Stout crossties of hardwood, partly hand-shaped, were easy to come by. On the banks beside the right of way grow laurels, protected by West Virginia law. Leathery-leafed rhododendrons were, gandy dancers admitted, pretty but a darned nuisance in rail work. Though this line, subject to change due to cutting of hardwood, wound into the wilds, concentrations of industry were close at hand. The manufacturers of steel, iron, glass, tanned leather and lampblack are extensive in the state, which, surprisingly enough, also ranks as agricultural. Corn is a leading crop. Only a third of West Virginia is improved. Obviously, the accompanying scenes are a part of the remaining two-thirds.

Rail historians found the stored equipment at Dundon of paramount interest. (BELOW) Shay No. 19 is in the process of replacing the No. 12 on the far track during an afternoon tinged with nostalgia, a rare element of the crewmen's work day.

Widen, a village at the Clay County line in central West Virginia, knew the smoke and commotion of many an Elk River coal train, but the 550 residents knew better than to complain. One does not despair of the ranking industry, for as long as it were there, the fortunes of Widen would not be thin. (BELOW) Rod engines, some acquired from as far away as the Savannah & Atlanta, let their presence be known in metropolitan Widen.

Elk River No. 17, a thin, second-hand Mikado, hurries along a load of coal waste to a dump — the natives call it a gob pile — outside of Widen. The train has just left a washing device. In years past, Buffalo Creek & Gauley ran passenger service into Widen. It was well patronized. Highway engineering in the area had not reached full potential.

BUFFALO CREEK & GAULEY

The mission of the Buffalo Creek & Gauley, up until its demise in the mid-sixties, was to take empties from the Baltimore & Ohio at Dundon, West Virginia,
to the coal mine at Widen, and to return the cars loaded to the Capitol Route.
Between the two BC&G extremities was Swandale as shown above, where the
two more industrious agencies were a lumber firm's company store and the mill
itself, over which towered three tautly braced smokestacks. BC&G's No. 4, built
new for the railroad, cuts through the middle of town on its way to the mine.

Consolidation No. 4, on the left, rarely sneaked into Swandale. In the illustration below, 2-8-0 No. 14, a makeover New York Central eight-wheel switcher, curves past the steep, steep sides vying with Ben Lomond.

BC&G motive power was maintained with finesse such as hostler Bobby Carruthers afforded. (RIGHT) No. 4 between Dundon and Cressmont where once was located the company dairy.

Any railroad is the combination of foresight, finance, friendly fortune and men and equipment. The BC&G was all of these and something else, as well. It had Richard Manning. One would be more than naive if Superintendent Manning were overlooked in the railroad's final stages. With little to summon for his disposal, Manning unquestionably did the most and No. 4, shown above, would not have performed as satisfactorily had not Manning been on the job more than he was required. As BC&G kept steam power such as the No. 14, shown in the upper right, center, well after other railroads, it was courted by photographers and magazine editors whose previous coverage had touched only on some vexing labor troubles. John P. Killoran, a loyal son of Marshall University, corrected this tarnished image by serving as volunteer BC&G press agent. He was joined by electrical firm draftsman William E. Warden who indited plentiful prose anent BC&G for public print. It was here at Dundon, at the upper right, that Andrew Wittenborn and Frank Barry concluded a trip from Colorado in a 1929 Graham-Paige, their rolling residence for many months. The Nos. 14 and 13, off the Kelly's Creek & Northwestern, were dashing additions to their photo array. The No. 13, at the right, became a weekday caller at Widen, lovingly referred to as the Widen place on the road, after the twice daily and once on Sunday passenger service was curtailed.

MEADOW RIVER

In 1906, two Ohio brothers named Raine withdrew from their logged-thin retentions in Pennsylvania to begin investment in 75,000 acres of hardwood in Greenbrier County, West Virginia. In four years, John and T. W. Raine were under way to presiding over their Meadow River Lumber Company, a triple band saw mill regarded as the largest hardwood enterprise of its kind in the entire world, one capable of providing 110,000 board feet daily. In a burst of admirable manufacture, it once turned out 206,000 board feet from sunrise to sunset. By 1913, a town—to which the Raines contributed generously—developed adjacent to the lumber yard. It was named Rainelle in honor of the lumbermen who insisted company houses for employes be of comfort, what with running water, electricity and certain indoor conveniences. At one time the Raines interests backed a 20-mile railroad, Sewell Valley, through commercially untouched terrain in meeting with the Chesapeake & Ohio. One SV locomotive eventually went south to the Rockton & Rion. Meadow River Lumber penetrated the wilds, too, with several geared engines. Among them was a Shay numbered 7, shown at the left, which after displacement by newer concepts, left Rainelle on a deputation of grandeur. No. 7 smartly painted, usurped the C&O right of way in traveling to Cass, West Virginia, for a stint as a people puller on the Cass Scenic Railway.

The expedition to Cass attracted a felicitious gathering. The Chesapeake & Ohio assigned a sympathetic crew of some stature: a superintendent, a trainmaster and a road foreman of engines. Among the photographers on that marrow-chilling December 8, 1964, were New Yorker John Krause, Richmonders D. Wallace Johnson and Bill Stratton and two of West Virginia's finest, the John Killorans. In addition, unsuspecting locals, of which is represented above a segment of Springdale, West Virginia, ran off the highway to examine such a specimen. (RIGHT) Years and years before the delivery to Cass, the No. 7 had been tidied early one morning, just as it was at Rainelle for a trip over from its former West Virginia workplace of Honey Dew. On the most recent time, the dew was frozen although the No. 7 benefitted by the touch of Carolyn Killoran who, 'tis said, undertook the man's job of applying new Cass tender stencils herself.

It's housecleaning time for Meadow River No. 5 after a day's logging. In the background No. 3 moves up with a work train near Anjean, West Virginia. (BELOW) On Election Day 1956, Shay No. 3's crew voted to get back to the mill in a hurry for lunch.

Scholars reporting on the activities of Shay No. 5, skidder and log loader, interpret this November 1956 scene as habiliment. Meadow River lumbermen saw it simply as devilishly hard work. (BELOW) Shay No. 5 runs to Anjean with a log load to transfer to Heisler No. 6 bound for Rainelle.

MOREHEAD & NORTH FORK

When Morehead & North Fork's Nos. 14 and 12, shown below, occupied top echelon on the motive power roster, the four-mile freight – only Kentucky railroad, listed itself in droll fashion in the Official Guide: "Morehead to Clearfield and beyond." What the M&NF meant by the great beyond was Summit, a mined cargo-loading point up a grade considered an obstacle for the former Union and Southern six-wheel switchers. Also leading to the Summit chute was a trail, well weeded and mud puddled, about the most flattering description it merits. At the time the No. 14 was a tenant in the Clearfield engine house, a curiosity once the possession of Kanawha, Glen Jean & Eastern shared a second track. The No. 14's shedmate, a 2-6-2, displayed a memorable Baldwin builder's serial: 33333. With road number of 11, the Prairie later went from the clay and pipe-hauling M&NF to the Everett tourist railroad in Pennsylvania.

Morehead & North Fork No. 14 (nee-Union No. 77) works an exchange of cars with the Chesapeake & Ohio at Morehead where its tracks border the campus of the State College, producer of scholars and whiz-bang basketballers. Shop facilities for the M&NF were at Clearfield, a community served adequately by a coliseum-sized IGA chain food store and a village pump yielding water nearly as tasty as that from the town well at Cliffside, North Carolina.

KENTUCKY & TENNESSEE

In the pocket of the Blue Grass State where coal mining and Mother Maybelle recordings are important to the welfare of the people, steam locomotives of the Kentucky & Tennessee served Stearns, Worley, Comargo, Blue Heron and the place named for the residence of Frank L. Baum's fictional wizard, Oz. In all, K&T mileage nearly reached 10. Stearns was distinguished by a homey hotel, a line of vintage railroad postcards at the corner drug store, a testimonial billboard to the goodly name of founder Justus P. Stearns and a K&T track leading to the Southern on which the short line's No. 10, a Mikado, bellows in the scene below.

With the Cincinnati, New Orleans and Texas Pacific tracks swinging up and away at the left, Kentucky & Tennessee No. 10 leaves a string of hoppers at Stearns for the Southern subsidiary.

Leaving the Stearns engine house and switching on the way to the Southern, the No. 11 waves Santa beard exhaust into Christmas card weather. When its servitude on the K&T was at an end, the doughty 2-8-2 underwent a series of stress tests heavily masked with security at Fort Eustis in Virginia, yet when the summer 1965 demolition attempts concluded, it was no secret that the steam engine could still run.

Kentucky & Tennessee No. 12, shown above, running beside the Cincinnati, New Orleans & Texas Pacific tracks at Stearns, is in familiar surroundings. It was a one-time Southern engine. (RIGHT) The No. 12 backs over Yamacraw bridge, the largest concrete structure of its kind when built.

More than appreciation of fresh air prompts the trainman to sit upon the pilot beam. He looks out for fallen rocks.

Running briskly in a secluded realm is the No. 11, glistening in the early sun. The structure on back of the tender in the view below was to protect trainmen from the elements. K&T men referred to it as a dog house. It was called something else by the more rascally farmfolk lacking, at their own domain, indoor necessities.

A way of life is slipping away from Stearns, Kentucky. The town hotel, embrac-
ing the mannerisms of an overgrown boarding house, the musty frame stores
downtown and the huffy-puffy steam engine leaving in the morning — they're
becoming scant reflections now in long-reaching memories.

EAST TENNESSEE & WESTERN NORTH CAROLINA

When considering the East Tennessee & Western North Carolina narrow gauge, it becomes trying when sifting fable from fact. The annoying result, albeit pleasant, is that if one searches Tweetsie legend long enough, it invariably proves out true. ET&WNC was the miniscule line with the flair for human nature, abetted in the main by conductor Cy Crumley, a countryman turned railroader who, during the Depression, permitted the needy to ride free. After all, the train was going their way. Tweetsie became many things in many ways to the mountaineers. It was after a fashion, a friend in their midst, but as old companions must, (LEFT) Tweetsie made a last round of visits from Elizabethton, Tennessee, on October 16, 1950. Railroad authority Jack Alexander, in cab, was among those from afar on the final run of ring-stacked No. 11. (ABOVE) Past each farm, Tweetsie would pass groups of sturdy souls, each having fought floods, forest fires, droughts, hard times and war days dry-eyed beside their cherished narrow gauge. Today, there were tears.

ET yards at Johnson City
parallel Clinchfield tracks.

All of Tweetsie did not die. Economically feasible was a nine-mile standard gauge industrial undertaking between Johnson City and Elizabethton, Tennessee. A pair of heavy 2-8-0's, secured from the Southern, replaced older hand-me-downs. In the illustration below, No. 207 switches a chemical materials plant at Port Rayon in 1963.

The No. 208 passes the
company's Johnson City
trucking facility.

Tweetsie engines always functioned well and looked resplendent. Here is one reason why.

Lest there be slippage, the No. 207's sand dome is filled.

BLACK MOUNTAIN RAILROAD

North Carolina's Black Mountain Railroad greeted New Year's Day of 1956 with a bit of vigorous doings on a two-mile branch to Bowditch. (UPPER RIGHT) Burnsville was sanctuary of the No. 3, an inheritance from the Clinchfield with which it was connected. (RIGHT) The 10-wheeler crossing Kona trestle, replaced another used 4-6-0, one it might be noted, that had for its former northern owner taken the first load of supplies into Johnstown, Pennsylvania, after a renowned inundation there. The BM's line, in addition to the foregoing points, also served Backus, Micaville and Windom.

94

SMOKY MOUNTAIN RAILROAD

Had Jay Gould scrutinized the fiscal docket of the Smoky Mountain, he would likely have uttered phrases thoroughly unsuitable here. The SM, poor, beloved old thing, was the subject of so many abandonment rumors that it had no other choice but to quit so as not to be construed as an agent of story-telling. Over wiggly rails whose sleepers slumbered under a cover of greenery, the No. 110 gamely set out from Knoxville — at the base of the University of Tennessee stadium — for Sevierville, a scant 30 miles away but an all-day endeavor at best. Were it not for Jack Foster, who kept SM running on a promise, a lick and undiluted sagacity, the former logging Pacific would have suffered prematurely a severe case of offal. Whatever Foster's pecuniary returns from the company were, they hardly covered his services. In the scene below, the signet-stacked engine has as its train a revenue oil car and a combine, empty save for conductor Ike Linebarger and his coop of chickens which registered no great protest about the frequent rides. The line's rail was such that the No. 110 seldom ran at speeds designed to pull a settin' hen off its nest,

BRIMSTONE RAILROAD

In the Tennessee province of New River where good order is kept by Deputy Sheriff Lindsay Sexton, Brimstone No. 35 delivers newly mined coal to the Southern Railway. One of the burghers, exhibiting little regard for becoming conduct, clambored aboard the Shay on a nefarious occasion, a shotgun clenched in his hand containing the finger best suited for the curvature of the trigger. The Brimstone crewmen, wisely seeking refuge at such a distance where they were unable to detect presence of a bullet in the barrel, summoned the services of peace officer Sexton who thereupon restored harmony by a well executed swat upon the intruder's head with a stoking shovel. Upon removal of a cylindrical object from the throat of the firearm, Sexton reminded the Brimstone crew that railroading was a hazardous occupation.

Shay No. 35 tops a hill overlooking a large lumber mill, New River's ranking industry in years past. (BELOW) The shops look a little soiled, but the two Shays seldom did. Crewmen even swept clear footboards and cab decking after each trip to the coal mines.

Recently painted No. 35 is replenished with coal, and the tender will soon receive yellow striping and lettering. (RIGHT) A caboose was a luxury Brimstone missed.

Often the No. 35 split its train to bring it piecemeal up the hill on the left. (RIGHT) A load of coal is placed for Southern pickup. (BELOW) The No. 35 roars down the main line, an inevitable lube tin sitting on the pilot beam.

You can lead an iron horse to water, and if you have a syphon, you can make it drink. Creek water and hose saved the expense of a tank.

Prior to the development of coal pursuits, the line traveled by the No. 35 had been given to logging. (BELOW) Though the Shay's way up is steep, the phased-out lumber yard manually operated railroad was worse. Cables were necessary there.

In upper Tennessee ran a humble coal road with a hellacious name: Brimstone. No. 36, one of the two final Shays, drops downgrade for a second portion of its load at New River.

At this late hour of steamdom, how many other locomotives were as well groomed as Brimstone No. 36? (BELOW) In Scott County of Tennessee, the Brimstone would fire up a Shay and light out 13 miles to a coal mine location, the identification of which generally escaped cartographers preparing filling station maps. The backwoodsy line, halting at a classic dead end, became even deader when forestry as well as coal yield dissipated. When the mine at the extreme reaches was productive, the Georgia-Pacific-controlled Brimstone ran rather regularly. Placement of cars on sidings along the line determined the locomotive's position in the train. No more than a raccoon's canter from where the photograph was made is located one of the nation's more modest food stores, tended by a housewife and located in a corner of her front porch. The wares are limited, of course.

Brimstone No. 36 lifts exhaust past mistletoe in the tree on the gentle slope behind the Shay. Summits at New River, to which the train is headed, are so steep that once railroad men were obliged to bring in new locomotives by means of a cable stretched from peak to peak. Remains of a Shay so imported was stripped to the frame, and with freight bogies slipped beneath, did admirably for years as a flat car.

GRAHAM COUNTY RAILROAD

In the Divine Order of things, Graham County Railroad made out tolerably well. It was located in one of the last untouched stands of hardwood. It benefitted from intelligent management, being linked to the lumber firm of Bemis. It had a pair of Shays which, upon observing their 40th birthdays, were hanging together commendably. While the immense grades on the line running from Robbinsville, North Carolina, to Topton where it interchanged with the Southern Railway's Murphy Branch were originally considered operating setbacks, the Graham County eventually found the Nantahala Gorge an asset when it courted tourist attention. In counting blessings, Graham County could also point squarely at its engineer, Ed Collins, a giant of a man imbued with human understanding. Ed's Shay steamed with more hospitality per square inch than most any other locomotive in the land. Bemis could hardly have hired a public relations man to better

the good will job Ed did. For one thing, Ed had an acute understanding of why people wished to photograph outdated steamers. That, within itself, won respect of many who, it follows, would talk up Bemis products. Ed had cut sharply around this Topton turn thousands of times, and for years it was merely a job. He assessed himself as a man who'd been obliged to leave his one-room frame school far too early to become a man of letters. He had to get a job aboard the Shays and that is where he'd stayed. With this background, all of a sudden Ed surprisingly emerged as a sort of a hero. Here was bighearted Ed presiding over an old-fangled steam engine on a story book line. It got so that people would come from all over the nation to see Ed and his Shays at the gorge, and Ed allowed as to how if being famous meant having so much company, it would do all right.

With a 50-gallon petroleum drum converted to a spark arrester over the smoke-stack, Ed and fireman Posey Davis bring a tank car from the Southern upgrade near Topton on a line once canvassed by a motor locomotive salesman. Upon noting the acclivity as well as the track, the wisest element of his persuasion contained itself in a single word: Goodbye.

The Robbinsville-Topton round trip can be negotiated in a half a day's time, depending how much of it is made on top of the rails. When the No. 1926 (wearing another engine's number plate when its own disappeared) and a tank car slid to the ground, it calls for a meeting of minds. (UPPER RIGHT) In the middle of the group, talking to superintendent G. L. Wilson is conductor C. C. Bateman, unruffled by the likes of this. Bateman, a genial host to callers himself, had seen far worse in his career dating back to when he was on speaking terms with the logging patriarch of them all, W. M. Ritter. The mishap was at eight in the morning and by four that afternoon, a samaritan with a bulldozer righted matters, marking Graham County's brief departure from steam-only ranks. Well, the track is in right fair shape in the view above, and Ed is fixing to run over to Topton as he always did, only a little tardier than normal.

With fearsome ejection smothering the cab, Ed throttles his charge past a safety track at Topton in the view above. Ed parks his Shay and walks by the fence to pass the time of day with a road gang on the job in a flanged-wheel Model A Ford in this, Krause's first Graham County photograph (Spring 1956). (RIGHT) In The Land of the Sky, Ed peeps about in low-flying clouds.

Ed rests his shovel on the gate of the coal bunker in the scene above. Running a Shay is work, but nothing compared to posing for pictures at the Robbinsville coal dock and, yes, that, is, indeed, track up there. (UPPER RIGHT) Past the weighing station and the coaling facility goes the Shay for another day, a Big John wood chip car hulking above the rest of the train. (BELOW) Railroaders on the pulp car drop off ties on a 1960 outing.

Graham County's conversational piece was its caboose, since having lost much of its character but gaining a fresh coat of paint and new timbers here and there. (LEFT) Running tender-first to Topton, No. 1926 pulls a democratic train — two box cars from a rug plant at Robbinsville and a like number of cars from the Bemis mill. (BE-LOW) The No. 1925 — numbered for the year it was built — cuts through the church grounds at Bear Creek where the U. S. Park Service, Bemis, Fontana Village, Government Services, Inc., and Graham County Railroad would erect an operating lumber mill, a depot and a haven for vacationers.

3 - The Deep South

EXPLORED EARLY by the Spanish, claimed by the French and held by the English, Alabama was ceded to the United States in 1783, developing into a cotton market after the War of 1812, when Andrew Jackson's forces repulsed Indians with finality. The ensuing Civil War drained Alabama. Recovery was tedious and slow. It would have been impossible without the railroads, including the short lines of a far later period showing in this work: Tuskegee, Birmingham & Southeastern, Sumter & Choctaw, Twin Seams, Mobile & Gulf and Alabama Central, lines rooted through the rural state still 60 percent forested.

In nearby Georgia, in this rail grouping steamed the Talbotton on its reserved — yet hectic — way.

Over the border is Mississippi, French-developed before 1700 and made a state in 1817, and severely restrained since the destruction of the plantation network after the Civil War. It is little wonder that the Magnolia State's railroads have had difficult going, for Mississippi has been bothered by the lowest national income and highest illiteracy, not to mention soil erosion. The competent Mississippian is a bright exception. Nearer the norm might be the Canton & Carthage, the Bonhommie & Hattiesburg Southern and the Crosby Wood Products firm, utilizing for many years the services of a well worn Shay.

Below Mississippi is Louisiana, the parcel of acres figuring in a publicized purchase by the United States in 1803. Included here are the Willis Short line, a gravel hauler of abbreviated trackage accurately defined in its business title, the Red River & Gulf and Tremont & Gulf, tapping oil supplies in the humid, sub-tropical state where tempers boiled even higher during Reconstruction.

A neighbor, Arkansas, looked over in 1541 by that master of wanderlust De Soto, went through French control before being lumped into the Louisiana Purchase and admittance to the Union in 1836. Entirely within the Mississippi River drainage basin, pocked with lakes and the Ouachita and Ozark highlands, Arkansas is represented photographically by the Murfreesboro & Nashville; Graysonia, Nashville & Ashdown; Prescott & Northwestern; Reader and Arkansas pikes, each in its own way, contributing to the movement of oil, cotton, bauxite, grain and wood products of the Razorback State.

Smoking out bleary eyed hootie owls from a decaying tree trackside, Prescott & Northwestern No. 7 leaves its mark over the Arkansas countryside. Since serving the P&NW, aligned with the Ozan Lumber Co., the 2-6-2 was acquired in 1961 by the Black Hills Central, a South Dakota people-totin' railroad between Keystone and the roaring fast town of Oblivion.

TALBOTTON RAILROAD

Talbotton's afflictions ranged from boll weevils looking for a home to the wearing out of men and their hand-me-down engines. Mostly, it was financial blight finally strangling the plucky seven-mile railroad a toot northwest of Albany, Georgia, in Talbot County. The line went in during 1872, principally to move out corn crops, which failed. Cotton replaced them and weevils took over from there in the twenties with the Depression coming on as an afterthought. In 1937, the Hampton Lumber Co. revived the timber business to lessen the crises. Central of Georgia leased Talbotton its venerable (Baldwin, June 1891) 4-4-0 No. 349 and even that had known a change or two in its time: Originally lettered Savannah & Western and numbered 557 until 1894 when it became Central of Georgia 1587; to 1581 in 1912; to 349 in 1926, and some pessimists intimated it went to pot when it struck Talbotton duty.

Hoving into Junction City, Georgia, Talbotton's No. 403 pauses for water. The former Sylvania Central 1905 Baldwin hangs on a while longer with stays from the cab to the catwalks. Talbotton engineer Mike Greathouse reckoned he had put in more than 400,000 miles which is something on a seven-mile railroad. On Mike's train much of the time was an open-end passenger coach, a wooden vehicle whose number and ancestry were obscured as were some of it s windows, being boarded up. Yet, the car did have a relief from formal railroad block lettering stencils in a gay freehand that served the purpose.

It was only natural that Talbotton be corrupted into Tall-bottom and for those whose responsibility it was to fill the tender with coal, there were days they wondered if it were not Tallbottom, indeed.

TUSKEGEE RAILROAD

As the crow flies — or brass eagle in considering Tuskegee's No. 101 — it was six miles from the railroad's namesake to Chehaw, Alabama. Among the trainmen on a return from a meet with the Western of Alabama at Chehaw is a denimed fellow with well developed curiosity. (RIGHT) Components of an authentic Dixie stump jumper manifest themselves in the Tuskegee Baldwin: The eagle perched askew atop the number plate, a melodious chime whistle, artful bolt heads on the pilot beam (one of which has been replaced by a more utilitarian style), brass candlesticks, a bell activated by cord rather than mechanically, a rotund engine master and a court of locally recruited aides, most of whom found constant delight in being photographed along with the locomotive.

BIRMINGHAM & SOUTHEASTERN

With a headlight nearly of carousel propor-
tions, Birmingham & Southeastern No. 200
added a note of distinction to daily trains
21-22-27-28 back in the days when the
Alabama shortline was a running outfit.
The engine, really too good to scrap, gained
a reprieve with a Vermont line subscribing
to people traffic. The Birmingham road was
incorporated in 1901 as Union Springs &
Northern and developed 48.2 miles from
Union Springs to Electric, Alabama, and
purchased in April 1912 the Tallassee &
Montgomery Railroad from Tallassee to
Milstead. By the early twenties, B&SE
counted four s t e a m e r s in its stable.
(RIGHT) When Southern short lines could
neither afford nor spare steam power from
revenue freight, passenger accommodations
often were less than esthetic as evidenced
by Birmingham & Southeastern's Edwards
motor car No. 502. Still, it did keep the
good folks of Tallassee, Tuckabatchie and
Milstead, Alabama, close in touch.

Sumter & Choctaw, working two regular crews, sometimes was so busy it summoned a make-up gang typified in the scene above by Connie Thomas, left, and Joe Evans on the pilot deck and the incomparable "Catfish" Ward wearing the latest in cat hats. Behind the pulp car is the slaughterhouse used for rendering lard in the series of conflicts categorized as World War II. (UPPER RIGHT) Around the Bellamy, Alabama, commissary where sooner or later everyone goes, the oldsters lean against the green frame walls and swap stories about the Sumter & Choctaw Railway mudline days. That was when the 102, of Baldwin logging design, dragged timber from the stands near the offshoot line south of Allison Lumber Co.'s sawmill. Why, engineer Charlie Steinwinder worked on the ground sometimes and let Willie "Catfish" Ward take charge of the engine called "steamwinder" in rhyming with Steinwinder's name. Remember old Percy Tidmore the fireman, a giant of a man who, the natives say, was plumb-near as strong as the No. 102 in his day? Then, there was that loader that tilted precariously when Charlie was in a rush. Now, Charlie's dead. The engine's gone. Place ain't the same. About here, the grayheads get dry in their throats. "Mudline times?" one would broach. "Let's drink to that. Here, son. Take this quarter and buy us a round of R.C.'s."

SUMTER & CHOCTAW

Reincarnation of a Southland short line engine added much to the total of the afficionado's happiness when Middletown & New Jersey, a tourist line, rehabilitated Sumter & Choctaw's 2-6-2 No. 103 which thereby was spared from accumulating more rust and vines at its storage track at the Bellamy, Alabama, yards of American Can Company. Jersey rejuvenators thoughtfully included floppy white extra flags, once in vogue for unscheduled runs. (LOWER LEFT) Though the Sumter & Choctaw surroundings of tall pines and delicately scented honeysuckle cannot be duplicated in 103's new theater of operations, the Jersey hillocks do offer admirable substitution.

TWIN SEAMS

In the yellow dirt and coal land of Alabama, Twin Seams Mining Co.'s Shay No. 8 toils cautiously over uncertain rails burrowed into the crags near Kellerman. Once through, the venerable locomotive smokes sinfully in shuttling about with mined goods for transfer to the Gulf, Mobile & Ohio.

Twin Seams' No. 8, a Cyrano de Bergerac of an engine, blows its nose. The enormous stack, whose derivations can be traced to Messrs. Radley and Hunter in 1850, housed a spark restrainer so the Shay wouldn't burn up the countryside. Near the top of the funnel was a plate for live sparks to strike (and dead ones, too). A cap at the bottom was opened, a pipe inserted and the leavings rolled clear of the front wheels.

The Shay, a strange looking, slow-moving vehicle, motivated by one-sided vertical piston rods, got by handily on poor rail and slightly less than minimum pampering with maintenance confined largely to sweat and swear. Yet the Shay lasted. Why, Twin Seams No. 5 was originally ordered by Winchester & Western in Virginia. Proving unsuited for that railroad, it was sold to the Meadow River Lumber Co. in West Virginia, spending a full career there. By the time the Alabama coal mining firm acquired the engine, it was just broken in good. (LEFT) In strip mining country, the rule of the road was for coal trucks to be driven on the hillside rather than the cliffside so as to avoid a tragic tumble in case of a collision. Motorists viewing Twin Seams No. 5's impromptu repair base for the first time were oft befuddled and short of breath after introduction to such driving rules. (RIGHT) The countenance of the Shay is likened unto one watching a tennis match. Side-glance boiler allowed room for the propulsion apparatus on the engineer's side. The engine's face was hardly Hollywood. It lacked painted makeup.

A pioneer Operation Head Start provided sanded traction for the geared engine whose drive wheels seldom slipped but when they did, it was en masse. (UPPER RIGHT) A starting point for the exhaust pattern of Twin Seams No. 8 may have been the wrath of the Almighty. The Shay's actual progress was measured with far less gusto. When the erstwhile Alabama & Tombigbee machine topped 10 miles an hour, the brakie up front just knew that was next to flying. (LOWER RIGHT) Beyond doubt, Mr. Ephriam Shay devised his famed contrivance to do maximum labor at minute expense. That his product was fascinating to see was secondary. When photographed near Kellerman, Alabama, by the likes of John Krause, Twin Seams No. 8 appeared in an aura of beauty — an individualistic pulchritude, at any rate.

In classic "I think I can, I think I can" setting, the little engine that could strives upgrade and past a pond toward Kellerman. (BELOW) Down the road apiece is the Kellerman post office tended by a postmistress intrigued with the attention outlanders gave the Twin Seams Shays. Camera addicts signed her guest registry, whose ruled pages bespoke of an earlier use as a ledger. Now that No. 8 has run its last over the trestle, the book is all but neglected.

Look sharply, now: This is a locomotive shop and fuel terminal. No costly flooring, no walls, no roof and the outlay for tools was modest, too. In the main, a maul and a welding torch would keep the old No. 5 going. Water, fed from a spout, was stored in a tender, stripped of its wheels, astraddle the hill. Coal, in copious supply nearby, was installed in the Shay by means of a time honored, rudimentary device — the shovel. (BELOW) Had the fates been more charitable, Twin Seams would have been running Shay No. 5 from the mines longer than the early sixties when railroading ceased. The Shay faithful may derive some degree of solace from knowing the end was not caused by engine failure. Rather, it was a bridge that caved in.

Mobile & Gulf, indispensable adjunct of the W. P. Brown & Sons Lumber Co. in Tuscaloosa County, deploys a charming labor practice: The engineer leaves the locomotive in his back yard. This way, he does not have far to go to work. (RIGHT) There was another 97 — on the Southern — that went downgrade making 90 miles an hour. Mobile & Gulf's No. 97 proceeds at far more cautious pace, one that will guard against a wreck such as Joe Broady's train 97 took at Danville, Virginia, a half-century previously.

MOBILE & GULF

Near the shores of the Sipsey River stretch 11 of Alabama's 5,500 railroad miles. The state claims one train mile for every nine and one-half square miles, while Mobile & Gulf's main aim is to get from Brownville to Buhl. It gave up long ago trying to make it to Mobile in the southern part of the state. Still, it had tried. Mobile & Gulf fell short of Mobile by only 150 miles. The Gulf of Mexico may have been another 40 or so beyond.

The little road then, is content with its brief span, following a custom of steam energy in a state imbued with tradition. In Mobile & Gulf's formative days, some Alabama wives were expected to walk 10 paces behind their husbands, including on trips to women's voting league meetings. Now, the comely Southern belles may be just a step ahead.

All the while, Mobile & Gulf's No. 97's seldom publicized movements revealed on these pages take it through a portion of the Cotton State, whose annals are, to be sure, vivid, for this is De Soto country — land that fluctuated between Spanish and French rule. The port of Mobile, the place Mobile & Gulf missed, was even once the capital of Louisiana.

ALABAMA CENTRAL

A unique grade crossing sign protects Alabama Central's No. 29, a 208,000-pound 2-8-0 with a coal load in from the mine at Jasper. The Richmond product of September 1923 was well traveled. It had been No. 35 on both Birmingham Southern and Chattahoochee Valley, No. 29 on Onieda & Western in Tennessee and retained this numeral farther south. (RIGHT) Alabama Central's No. 29 knows not the impiety of stencils, displaying home-styled lettering that gave down-South lines an individuality missing elsewhere.

The nine-mile Jasper to Marigold line of Alabama Central depended on coal and when that was depleted, the No. 29 and second engine, at the far right, stopped interchange at Jasper with the Frisco, the Southern and the Illinois Central.

MISSISSIPPIAN RAILWAY

Four of the more prominent denizens of Amory, Mississippi, are the brothers Carlisle (Frank and James) and the two steam locomotives assigned to their care (76 and 77). The brothers, dutifully devoted to their railroading chores on the 24 miles to Fulton, take turns conductoring and engineering with their respective ex-Frisco 2-8-0's. (RIGHT) Here is the team peeping out of the No. 76 on a wintry day playing tricks on the Sunny South. (BELOW) When finished with flagging chores, the station master tells vivid tales of older Mississippian power to those who would listen and sometimes the Carlisles add a few first-hand tales of their own. The story on this day, however, is a dark one. (LOWER RIGHT) Mississippian is a rather long name to stencil, so an abbreviation was in order, prompting an untoward sobriquet of "Misery" and the far kinder "Miss Railway."

At night, Amory, Mississippi, is a quiet town with the mere chatter of the night bugs breaking the calm beside the sandy road to the Mississippian engine house. Only the two idled locomotives could cause a start, for the Carlisles have a game they foist on guests. "Which engine looks better?" one will ask. "Is mine neater than his?" chides the other. Partiality could be dangerous and, in truth, the brothers, admittedly attempting to outdo each other in upkeep and trim of the motive power, are happiest when the visitor calls the contest a draw. (UPPER LEFT) A Carlisle axiom: to regular lubricants, add a little elbow grease. (LEFT) Coal-burning Mississippian No. 77 starts its day with a flourish.

Dapper? There's no doubt of it. Reddened number plate, catching beads of nocturnal moisture, sets off the Mississippian No. 77 for a distinguished portrait beside the coal loader in front of the two-stall locomotive shed at Amory. (BELOW) When the Carlisles discovered the weed on the rail, it was certain to be uprooted. The Carlisles are not the type to let grass grow under their feet.

CANTON & CARTHAGE

Canton & Carthage in Mississippi ran its large — by short line South standards — 2-8-2 from Canton to McAfee, representing something like 35.75 miles and maybe more if switching was totted up as well. (UPPER RIGHT) Owing allegiance to forestry, Canton & Carthage No. 202 connected with Illinois Central at Canton on a right-of-way contrasting from that of the old I. C. Opposite this scene, the No. 201 "piping hot" rests for the next freight run. (ABOVE) Another popular feature of Southern wee lines was a large backup light on the cab roof. Hand-lettered Canton & Carthage No. 202 was equipped in accepted mode.

BONHOMIE & HATTIESBURG SOUTHERN

Bonhomie & Hattiesburg Southern's cap stacked 2-8-2 was, in proper perspective, a machine with which to move materiel for profit. Viewing it this way was not always that simple. Anyone with any emotion at all recognized the train in its rural Mississippi rounds as making for a deucedly pretty picture. A portion of the Mobile, Jackson and Kansas City Railroad, the line became the Hattiesburg branch of the Gulf, Mobile & Northern until the B&HS acquired it in September 1923, primarily for the lumber trade. (UPPER RIGHT) Trains 31 and 32 of the Bonhomie & Hattiesburg Southern were often in care of No. 250, an upright, proud-lined 2-6-2 slowing for a water stop. (CENTER) In the weeds inevitable, ventures Bonhomie & Hattiesburg Southern with what can be accurately described as full head of steam. (LOWER RIGHT) In keeping with the grand tradition, Bonhomie & Hattiesburg Southern's larger locomotive No. 300, a 2-8-2, is appointed with a mammoth spread eagle. The 1925 Baldwin leaves Beaumont, Mississippi, with sizable burden in 1957.

In the wintry fog of a November morning in 1960, each wetted pebble of the unpaved road outside Hattiesburg glistens as if a pearl in the glow of No. 250's headlight. (BELOW) Attesting to the warmth of the B&HS No. 250's engine cab are the brief, informal, iconoclastic attire of the crew as well as not one but two drinking water containers stacked on the tender. The 2-6-2 takes to a timber trestle on its way to Hattiesburg.

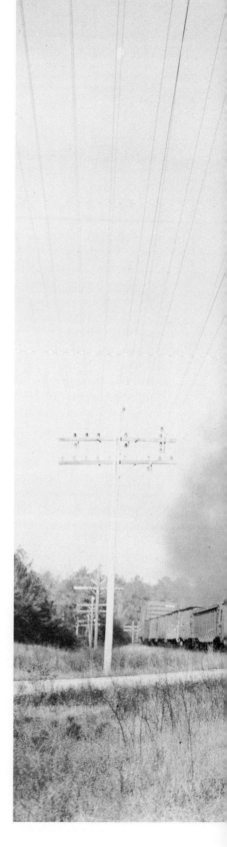

Making for Beaumont, Mississippi, bell flailing and smoke trailing, B&HS No. 250 heads into the twilight which might very well have been its own. Instead of a rendezvous with the junk man, the 1926 Baldwin was sent to a Pennsylvania tourist railroad, the Wanamaker, Kempton & Southern, utilizing an old Reading Company branch. There the engine, its eagle polished, began gaining even more widespread devotion from steam locomotive addicts.

CROSBY WOOD PRODUCTS

Crosby Wood Products' One Spot, a wood-burning Shay, shows the effect of many seasons: Pilot beam grabirons are bent, the glasses are gone from the headlight along with the bulb, the number plate is out of line — and what counts most? The engine runs and does all that is demanded of it. (LEFT) Its very antiquity earned the Crosby Shay a certain veneration by erudite editor William S. Young in his Steam Locomotive magazine. (LOWER) A man with a bit of wit chalked "Hoss" on the tender of the Crosby Shay, although the consequences may have been a trifle philosophical at that, for essentials of the old locomotive were kept in repair. Be it known, Crosby's crew may have been appalled had they known of careless Class I practices elsewhere in the nation.

WILLIS SHORTLINE

Outshopped by the Baldwin Works in 1889, the 10-wheeler of Willis Shortline Railroad Company, Inc., ranks as hardy. It still labored in the early 1960's at Enon, Louisiana. Total main line mileage was estimated at 250 yards with nearly 80 feet in sidings. The locomotive, at this late state, was one of few having to work while going downhill and pushing cars. (LOWER LEFT) Its latter day career spent with the Willis gravel interests, the No. 200 — showing lettering of Texas & Pacific influence — will be ready to go with a swat here and a slam there and an ignited match in the correct place. (BELOW) Willis Shortline's No. 200 was a whilom Cinclaire Central Factory sugar plantation switcher in Louisiana and before that was a Texas & Pacific property. Whether it supplied a racier photographic moment in years of yore is conjectural.

RED RIVER & GULF

Under ownership of Crowell Long Leaf Lumber, 10-wheeler No. 400, a February 1919 Baldwin, stands stack and shoulders above the belle of Long Leaf, Louisiana. The No. 202 withstood the ravages of modernity. It didn't even burn coal. (LEFT) Pushing the limits of credibility, Crowell Lumber's wood-burning, cabbage-stacked 2-6-0 No. 202 was real. Had Phineas T. Barnum himself viewed it in its Long Leaf, Louisiana, haunts, he would have registered hearty approval of the yellow and red paint scheme.

TREMONT & GULF RAILWAY

Smack in the middle of the swamplands of Louisiana was the Tremont & Gulf, whose orderly No. 44 running extra at the far right is representative. The T&G, initially chartered as a railroad in July 1902 and becoming a railway on December 18, 1907 and picking up the Shreveport, Jonesboro & Natchez the year previously, grew to a 72-mile routing. Tremont to Winnfield was 48¼ miles and Menefee to Rochelle was 18½ and branches made up the difference. Ten miles were sold in 1915 with abandonment pruning the rest. (ABOVE) Tremont & Gulf No. 25, outshopped at Matthias Baldwin's engine factory in August 1913, whirls its 54-inch drivers with a way freight near Winnfield, Louisiana, a metropolis from which three daily trains, including passenger service, emanated as late as the forties. Connections were effected with the Illinois Central's Yazoo & Mississippi Valley branch, the Rock Island and the Louisiana & Arkansas at various points. (RIGHT) In moving the output of oil and forest industries, Tremont & Gulf regularly directed its No. 28, a comely 2-8-0, to the line's zero milepost with the provocative name of Eros.

146

MURFREESBORO & NASHVILLE

An Arkansas traveler, Murfreesboro & Nashville No. 7 on the left, enjoys a 1951 day of admirable commerce. Had every work day been this profitable, the 1952 abandonment would have been avoided. (ABOVE) The very antithesis of the lonesome railroad whistle celebrated in song and poetry is No. 7's church organ chimes which tootled a cheery greeting even when intended to warn a body to get the devil out of the way. (TOP CENTER) Who'd have thought the slow train through Arkansas could set the woods on fire? Well, the Murfreesboro & Nashville did one January day in 1951. Good story that it is, No. 7 helped put a damper on it. (RIGHT) Months away from its final run, 2-6-0 No. 7 goes out in a burst of effulgence.

GRAYSONIA, NASHVILLE & ASHDOWN

Working under the florid banner of Graysonia, Nashville and Ashdown, No. 26 wends its reserved way through agrarian Arkansas during an era when coal smoke over light rail was the expected. (RIGHT) Mineral Springs on the O.K. Cement Route fell shy of Grand Central, maybe, but when it came to being picturesque, the Arkansas depot beat Gotham all hollow. (LOWER RIGHT) After a stint at meeting with Murfreesboro & Nashville, the Graysonia, Nashville & Ashdown's Baldwin 2-6-0 was sent far from its Arkansas hideaway to work for Ideal Cement's railroad, Nebraska-Kansas at Superior, Nebraska.

PRESCOTT & NORTHWESTERN

The Prescott & Northwestern, a 31.3-mile Arkansas concern with No. 7 as transportation agent, was the steam linking of Prescott and Highland via Tokio (Arkansas, i.e.). (BELOW) The main advantage of Prescott & Northwestern's motor car symmetry over the depot was its wheels. Curious pooches much preferred the shade beneath the station. (LOWER RIGHT) Prescott & Northwestern's own pronouncement in the Official Guide was "operations for irregular freight service only." One of the irregulars sees duty in the land of the razorbacks.

READER RAILROAD

The Possum Trot Line, whose corporate indentity is simply Reader Railroad, was using snorting Mogul No. 11 in 1950 to run tank cars from the Nevada County oil fields of Arkansas to a connection with the Missouri Pacific at the terminal from which the road drew its name. A compact little Alco product, Reader 401, a 2-8-0, is parked under dreary skies amidst castoff parts. Reader's picture was not bleak for long—T. W. M. Long, the Reader's president and general manager, headquartered at Shreveport, Lousiana. Long, alert to tourism values, did something unprecedented: He publicized Reader as a passenger caterer, becoming the only authentic steam powered mixed train operation in the United States, a fact given due prominence in the public press. (BELOW) When the Possum Trotters sailed from home base at Reader, they chuffed through such quaint points as Ada, Dewoody Spur, Cummings Springs, Dills Mill, Anthony Switch, Ames and Waterloo, the one alien to Monsieur Bonaparte.

ARKANSAS RAILROAD

Between the towns of Star City and Gould, the now abandoned Arkansas Railroad No. 150, a dachschund of a Mogul, works modest tonnage over a trestle on the 17.6-mile route. In true oil-burner fashion, fire flashes from its backside and a smear of white smoke leaks from its stack. The little train gives the appearance of having no place to go. Were it not for the fairly well established rail, maybe it wouldn't have. Surely, it was in no hurry. Half way out on the line, the crew stopped the engine and the men sought haven in the country store for coffee, preferred over big orange drinks this cold, damp day. The railroaders then repaired to their engine to head for whatever awaited them at Gould, where the conductor was much put out when there were no cars to pick up and the local freight 'way overdue. The men elected to return to Star City without waiting for the local. Tomorrow was another day. Trouble with the Arkansas road was it ran out of tomorrows.

4 · Main Lines
of the South

Beyond the realms of Dixie, Western Maryland, nevertheless, did occupy itself in terrain resembling that far lower in the Mason-Dixon territory. Under slate skies, a plump WM 2-8-0, the No. 830, lends reflection to a lake just outside of Thomas, West Virginia, a district with some built-in gradient problems.

CHESAPEAKE & OHIO's plush trains thundered down the trail of American Independence. The *Fast Flying Virginian*, the *Sportsman* and *George Washington* would bolt out of Washington in plunging into Virginia, the nation's historyland. On the coal line was Williamsburg, an erstwhile capital of the United States, and Hampton, the oldest continuous English-speaking settlement in the country (1610). Nearby are Jamestown, the first permanent settlement (1607) and Berkeley Plantation, site of the initial observance of Thanksgiving (1619).

Other Virginia mainline action chronicled here includes the Louisville & Nashville, also a heavy coal mover in the western part of the Commonwealth where mountains squeeze up acreage; the unheralded bituminous mover Interstate, and the dreadfully efficient coal transporter Norfolk & Western which changed character with its Virginia Creeper, a mixed dropping south from the Barter Theatre town of Abingdon, Virginia, to the pastoral terminal of West Jefferson, North Carolina.

In other ranges of the South are representative photographs of the Southern, Clinchfield, Central of Georgia, Seaboard, Atlantic Coast Line and Illinois Central, all far-flung general cargo handlers.

From the Southwest are the Rock Island, Texas & Pacific and the St. Louis-Southwestern.

In pre-script and gay color days, Chesapeake & Ohio ran conservatively handsome trains out of Alexandria, Virginia. The cars were dark green and gold-lettered in a style befitting the railroad image. The engine? The No. 482 looked good as a locomotive should. (LEFT) Southern's oil-burning "Joe Wheeler" honored an eminent son of the Old South, Confederate General Joseph Wheeler (1836-1906), for whom a town on the line in Alabama is named. Fightin' Joe, wounded three times in The War in Knoxville and Carolinas campaigns, recuperated to resume soldiering in the Spanish American War, notably at San Juan Hill where rough riding was in vogue. The motor car was similarly disposed, resulting in a short term on Southern's equipment roster.

Customary white flags mark Richmond, Fredericksburg & Potomac's No. 402 as an unscheduled movement at Alexandria, Virginia, in the late forties. In common with Chesapeake & Ohio's practice, pumps and headlight were placed up front leaving precious little room for the engine's number plate tucked in free space just under the headlight. RF&P deployed cast cabside numerals. (UPPER RIGHT) In the Commonwealth of Virginia, where the class of freight locomotive designated as Berkshire was especially well suited, Richmond, Fredericksburg & Potomac 2-8-4 No. 572 works a fast merchandiser at Alexandria. Other railroads in the state enjoying success with similar locomotives were the Virginian, the Chesapeake & Ohio and the Louisville & Nashville. (OPPOSITE) Lacking notoriety of other stellar Chesapeake & Ohio motive power, long and lean No. 2952 was assigned to local and catch-all trains at Alexandria in 1948. Without such yeoman service, C&O stockholders would not have fared so well at dividend time. (BELOW) Former Southern Railway President Fairfax Harrison fretted not over tradition. Seeing gaily colored locomotives abroad, Mr. Harrison ordered passenger power under his command in the Twenties to be painted Virginia green with gold trim. No. 1398 at Alexandria, Va., in 1948, was such a specimen, similar to the engine now displayed a few miles away in the Smithsonian Institution at Washington.

SOUTHERN RAILWAY

Where Virginia runs out of land in the Southwest, Southern Railway Mallet No. 4017 hurls a cloud of its own into an already gray November 1950 sky at the coal-oriented community of Appalachia. (UPPER RIGHT) North Carolina is a state plentiful with houses of higher learning and in the very midst of the educational climate is robust industry. Nearby Southern six-wheeler No. 1689 at High Point is the college bearing the city name as well as Elon, Greensboro College, Guilford and the Woman's College of the University of North Carolina. How the railway shopmen repaired the smokebox of the switcher is an education within itself, one obviously that did not originate from books. (BELOW) Two motor units of the railway that "Serves the South" bridge an Alabama valley.

CLINCHFIELD RAILROAD

A saving grace amongst some Clinchfield motor units was installation of air horns that were fair mimics of steam whistles.

INTERSTATE RAILROAD

Interstate No. 7 parallels Park Avenue of Norton, Virginia. The 2-8-0 heads for Andover on ground known in ante-iron horse times as Prince's Flat. Boyd J. Bolling of Flat Gap rued passing up purchase of the whole area for 50 cents an acre. People those days thought the place wouldn't amount to anything. (BELOW) Just before sundown at the Southeast Virginia mine municipality of Norton, one of Interstate's trim 2-8-8-2-'s would fight uphill on the way in from Appalachia. Freshly arrived, the No. 20 marshals hoppers to the Norton scales.

NORFOLK & WESTERN

Norfolk & Western trains 101-102, running their twisting way over bridge and through verdant dale from Abingdon, Virginia, to West Jefferson, North Carolina, resembled Dixie short line far more than the proper coal-hauling operation earning N&W its appellation of Precision Transportation. (BELOW) The old hand-fired 4-8-0, a turn of the century holdover, boasted a spark arrester stack suitable by Meerschaum standards. A pair of Tuscan red and gold-lettered coaches trail the mixed at Hungry Mother State Park, just down the line a-ways from Abingdon whereat is located the state theater named Barter. In Depression Days, dramatic patrons rode in on the Virginia Creeper train with country hams to swap for theater tickets. Theatergoers paid mostly cash for N&W tickets. (LEFT) Closely resembling another passenger engine, (the Norfolk & Western J) No. 122 — an older breed subsequently streamstyled — passes a hardworking Y on its infrequent venture east of Roanoke, Virginia. The Highway 460 underpass has since benefitted from a second bore.

Running boldly on the Norton, Virginia, to Bluefield, West Virginia, route, Norfolk & Western No. 578 was a beauty that begged to be photographed. It was even the subject of a commercial color post card. Now an Ohio museum piece, the engine is still a sightly subject for snapshooters.

By 1956, Norfolk & Western's Shenandoah Valley line offered an anachronism: a mixed train with a streamlined steam engine. To top it all off neatly, a caboose was appended to the train.

Late in the summer's day west of Bluefield, humidity is uncomfortable and back in the cab of Norfolk & Western No. 2135, it's worse.

WESTERN MARYLAND

In the decade before the War Between the States, industrious burghers of Union Bridge, Maryland, and Westminister — in the adjacency of Baltimore — were of the mind their trade would be expedited with introduction of the novel vehicles that moved about over metal rails. Accordingly, the route was surveyed in the proximity of where a pair of English astronomers, Charles Mason and Jeremiah Dixon, appraised a line along the 39-degree, 43-foot latitude the century before. It had settled a boundary dispute between Pennsylvania and Maryland, and would betoken regions north from south.

For a time, the railroad developing into the Western Maryland even called itself "The Mason-Dixon Line."

The City of Baltimore, during the early days, gained ownership. Jay Gould interests bought into the company in 1902 while the Baltimore & Ohio in 1927 gained control of the 800-plus-mile bituminous hauler (40 per cent of the business) that diversified into moving merchandise to the point of adopting a new slogan: "Fast Freight Line."

A steam era connection was with the Pittsburgh & West Virginia at Connellsville, Pennsylvania.

Western Maryland also delved into ore traffic.

Portions of the line were steeped with 3.8 percent grades, necessitating multiple powering as exemplified in the scenes below.

Western Maryland emblazoned in red on the tender, chunky 2-8-0 wins an uphill battle at Thomas, West Virginia, on a freezing day in 1962. (BELOW) Terrain of Thomas often required services of eight Western Maryland 2-8-0's on a single coal train. Two pushers of a four-locomotive move in 1952 work around a sharp bend pocked with lightly crusted snow. Far to the south, Southern Railway, meeting similar difficulties of gradient, was wont to couple three to five 2-8-0's on freight moving over its Murphy Branch west of Asheville in the "Land of the Sky" in North Carolina.

Bearing resemblance to the unsophisticated Virginian Railway No.'s 3 and 4 terminating in Tidewater, Virginia, Western Maryland's No. 209 dashes through McCoole, Maryland, in hill country with the Elkins-Cumberland people hauler. Two officials' cars at the end are extraordinary. In another sense, so was the passenger operation itself, returning a mere penny toward every Western Maryland dollar despite a retroactive postal contract. Yet, the unsullied trains were available to travelers in WM's spirit of benevolence that intruded little upon an operating ratio of 68 percent for the time.

In rusticana easily doubling for the Southern's Danville line outside of Richmond, Virginia, Western Maryland 2-8-0 No. 763 on a local freight heads north at a point just south of Gorman, Maryland.

Western Maryland No. 205, running a Sunday extra at Hancock, Maryland, lays out a vapor trail in an atmosphere removed from austral. (BELOW) Drifting into Cumberland, Maryland, is brutish boilered Western Maryland 4-6-6-4 No. 1204, almost passing for a Clinchfield articulated out of its Carolina environs.

CENTRAL OF GEORGIA

Tennille, Georgia, is cleft by Central of Georgia No. 614 on its June 29, 1949 run recorded on film much to the amusement of the conductor, engineer and attendant of the Texaco station built to familiar lines of yesteryear. (BELOW) Central of Georgia's No. 415 and three-car train halt at Rocky Ford, Georgia, to unload baby chicks while the connecting Sylvania Central switches rack cars to the rear. The Pacific type locomotive retains the old time flavor with brass eagle and fraternal emblem augmenting the front end and stars affixed to the silvered steam chests. It was on such an accommodation that many a disheartened Southland lover went down the track, weeping bitter tears at each clickity-clack and never, oh, never, to come riding back. Similar domestic pathos was expressed in the numberless songs of the folk down home. (LOWER RIGHT) Stack all but screened by a topside Elesco vertical coil feedwater heater, a Central of Georgia 4-8-2 awaits duty at Macon on June 17, 1949, an occasion abound with intense heat.

ATLANTIC COAST LINE

Ending long and useful service on the Atlantic Coast Line, towering 10-wheeler No. 1012 still managed a certain zip with Eastern North Carolina branch line trains that served such communities as Spring Hope, Parmele and Little Washington, once the home of no less a celebrity than movie mogul Cecil B. DeMille himself.

SEABOARD AIR LINE

The Seaboard engineer aboard the rollicking No. 310 tosses a hi-y'all wave in Deep South decor intensified with shreds of gray-green Spanish moss and the revered name of Leesburg, Florida.

LOUISVILLE & NASHVILLE

A brace of Louisville & Nashville 2-8-2's, on the left, the Nos. 1891 and 1914 in the lead, head through Powell River Valley in the western extremity of Virginia on The Old Reliable's Appalachia-Norton route criss-crossing the Interstate's path. (LOWER RIGHT) It's an easy road just now, but when the Mikes reach the water tank just outside Norton, it will be a long, hard pull. The L&N's newer Berkshires were known to slip and stall there. (RIGHT) Louisville & Nashville No. 195, first of 17 home-built Pacifics in 1912, cuts out of Appalachia, Virginia, with the Norton local.

ILLINOIS CENTRAL

Casey Jones' railroad has calmed down since the Vaughn, Mississippi, incident at the turn of the century. (RIGHT) On May 25, 1950, Illinois Central No. 2097 creates an ear-tingling racket through Silver Springs — but the safe passage missed entry into immortality via folk song. Casey made it by smacking into a caboose of another train. (ABOVE) In cornpone and magnolia premises, Illinois Central 2-8-2 No. 1434 takes hold of a gondola and pulp rack car train in a part of Mississippi feeling full effect of a sizzling May 1950 sun.

ROCK ISLAND

Rock Island No. 2694, perpetrating a generous pall of exhaust, is 278.2 miles out of Little Rock, Arkansas, but moving rapidly at Alexandria, Louisiana, to change that measurement on a May day of 1950. (BELOW) Like Joseph's coat of many colors, Rock Island motor combine No. 9070 comes cloaked in varied hues at Winnfield, Louisiana. Also on this particular Rock Island line were intermediate points Lillie, Bernice, Hilly, Clay, Turkey Creek, Pine Prairie and Mamou, each colorful in its own right.

ST. LOUIS SOUTHWESTERN

That tall-drivered engine No. 817 ran into Texarkana, Arkansas, as if the devil himself were stoking. The 1951 freight added lustre to the revenue sheets of the St. Louis Southwestern Railway Lines, more readily identified by its nickname, The Cotton Belt Route.

TEXAS & PACIFIC

Thin-stacked Texas & Pacific No. 359, a 10-wheeler of winsome lines, speeds a modest accommodation through Texas in January 1950.

Index